MASTERC

by the same author

♣

Music for Brass (Peterloo Poets, 1990)

Masterclass

BRIAN WALTHAM

PETERLOO POETS

First published in 1994
by Peterloo Poets
2 Kelly Gardens, Calstock, Cornwall PL18 9SA, U.K.

© 1994 by Brian Waltham

All rights reserved. No part of this publication may be reproduced, stored in a retrieval system, or transmitted, in any form or by any means, electronic, mechanical, photocopying, recording or otherwise without the prior permission in writing of the publisher.

A catalogue record for this book is available from the British Library

ISBN 1-871471-45-1

Printed in Great Britain by
Latimer Trend & Company Ltd, Plymouth

ACKNOWLEDGEMENTS are due to the editors of the following journals: *The Listener*, *New Statesman*, and *Spectator*.

INVESTMENT
SOUTH WEST ARTS

Contents

page
- 9 Yamahas at Milton Parva
- 10 Leafman
- 11 Visiting Time
- 12 Ginette Neveu
- 13 Supplement to a Sermon
- 14 Driving Home
- 15 Me and Descartes
- 16 Hitch-hiker.
- 17 Whortleberries
- 18 Rabbits at Harvest
- 19 Cattle Trucks
- 20 In the Pub
- 21 If You Have a Moment
- 22 Serum
- 23 Peace
- 24 Scaffolder
- 25 Coming of Age
- 26 Let It
- 27 Hospital Visitors
- 28 Crutchspeed
- 29 E.F.L.
- 30 Mandelbrot
- 31 With the Woolwich
- 32 Blake
- 33 'Do not go gentle into that good night'
- 34 Diatonic
- 35 Amanita Virosa
- 36 At the Ferry
- 37 Notre Dame des Touristes
- 39 Place de L'Opéra
- 40 Coffee at Montségur
- 42 Bon Marché

43	Castle Museum at Foix
44	Centre Ville
45	Cicadas
46	Masterclass
47	St. Francis in Tarn-et-Garonne
48	Downhill
49	Bardon Hill
50	Bardon
51	The Hall
52	Countryman
53	Whist
54	Aunt Nell
55	Aunt Nell's Legacy
56	Aunt Nell and the Album
57	Uncle George
58	For the Record
59	Actuarial You
60	Citadel
61	Care Home
62	In There
63	Wheelchair Meeting

Yamahas at Milton Parva

Headstone above leaning headstones,
You look good, you lovely tower,
You go well with green.
What, if you could be heard,
Would you tell us, a quarter
Past Cranmer, a quarter to
The Second Book of Kings?

Some say you lost it with the Tudors
And the rest was coercion.
Some say you lost it with Newman
And the rest was empire.
These bikes, snarling at your wall,
Might say you died on the Somme.

What, after the bitter centuries,
Can you say as they skirt you,
Hugging danger like a girl?
Idiots without history, but they have
Memories that are boundary marks,
Fields and ditches, stone that was
Here before you were built.
They know about stone.

Leafman

The leafman is singing.
With his two paddles he
Marries torn plastic, dog-ends,
Dogshit and leaves
And dumps them in his barrow.

Out of tune,
Pausing for bend and dump,
But he is singing and
Seeing me, he goes
On singing.

To get my Mercedes out
I have to wait for him
To move his barrow.

To get dogshit off a paddle
You have to scrape it
With the other paddle.
He takes his time and
Goes on singing.

Visiting Time

Suppose it's the other way round:
Not Dido wan among the shades,
But Pious Aeneas.
Suppose it's Dido, happily married
With four kids, who takes time off
To come down here.

Like all visitors, she
Brings snaps of friends, holidays
And gossip about what is
Going on up there.

But I think she will also be
More practical. She will bring
Foot-warmers, underworld underwear,
A new stock of pills and the special
Toothbrush that he can't get down here.
She will notice his pallor, remind him
About a balanced diet and, as he
Twists like a leaf in the thin wind,
Go on about the not-his children and
Wave cheerily as the bell calls time.

Ginette Neveu

(violinist, killed in the St. Miguel aircrash 1949)

May it be that, like the score
She was reading, the faltering whine,
The pitch and lurch, the tilt of sense,
Were all dynamics the music demanded.
May it be that just then she saw a
Phrasing, an up-bow hand across
Two strings and the same catch of breath,
The one note held on high F, waiting
For brass and timpani to have it their way.

As plane became leaf, may it be that
Among the cut and thrust of rehearsal
The last bleak commands were not
For her and that, out of habit, she
Touched her Strad strapped in beside her.

Then it can pass that she was just
Thirty-one and had those hands
And a face so lovely that
You stood and shouted
Before she ever played a note.

Supplement to a Sermon

Blessed also is he who,
Instead of crowding up here
On this Mount, stayed behind
And got on with his job,
Has a few close friends, gets
On with his wife, doesn't cheat
Over-much, is not loaded with guilt,
Laughs at a dirty joke, knows
My Father is around but doesn't
Need me to rub it in and couldn't
Spare the time to get here.

Blessed is he who, holding
Wet clay centred on the wheel
And yelling at his kids, will
Hear from you, crowding into his
Shop, my One And Only Truth and
Will smile in his own way
And go on treadling his wheel.

Blessed is he who down the
Centuries, house burnt, wheel
Broken for my One And Only Truth,
Will sit me out and, with no
Malice, wonder whether I might
Have stayed with saw, adze,
Plane, set-square, the mulish
Obstinacy of things to be made,
The ambiguity of grain in wood.

Driving Home

The shutter flicks at
The edge of just gone
And, watching the car ahead,
You name what you saw:
A slewed van, someone
Cradling a head, spilled
Shopping, Daz, Kelloggs,
Two oranges.

The radio tells you half
A million homeless in flood.
Fund set up ...

Two oranges.

And the kids, with Mum
Not back, raiding the
Biscuit tin and a slow
Stew on the hob and the
Ironing half-finished.

Me and Descartes

He decides to
Think about something.
I decide it's high time
I thought about something.

He sits right
Down and thinks.
I need first to feel
The pimple on the back
Of my neck.

He is distracted by nothing.
I notice two birds—no three—
Squabbling for a chimney pot.

He reaches an answer
And writes it down.
I add curlicues and
Arabesques to my doodle.

Hitch-hiker

Mid-forties, smart overnight bag,
Collar with a touch of blood on it,
Face I don't really look at.

His payment is to relax at
My driving, cuss the road-up cones,
Reach with questions I can duck:
All with the undertow that this
Is not what he's used to.

And there should be a reach back.
'So you're bound for Leicester?'
I should ask, but my blithe car
Has gone heavy and I too don't
Want the load of answer.

Two sorts of failure.
But when I've dropped him
I start singing idiot songs
At the top of my voice.

Whortleberries

They grew down the barbed wire quarry
Or overhung the river slope, fenced in
By briars. Then, as you clung there,
A spike in your hand for every one you got.

In Heaven there will be thick,
Well-made pastry, this morning's cream
And whortleberry pie.

Short of that, they're a sheer drop,
Toe searching for a hold, face in the
Smell of moss and down there the quarry floor
Or the river with its cold noise and
Dark among the underwater colour and
Birds shouting he'll fall he'll fall.

Rabbits at Harvest

First a machine round the field's edge.
Nothing much to worry about, but
Best to get in the middle.

Then families beginning to be
Jammed together, quarrelling,
Some foreign, some with burrows
To guard, and young bucks excited
And oldies who said it meant nothing.

Then the afternoon getting tall
With what couldn't happen and noise
Like childbirth and almost overhead
The cut and slash of blades, dogyelp,
Screaming, running, straw ghetto shrinking,
Fights at the burrows, oldies trampled
And the sky yelling 'there's plenty
Of 'em in there'.

Then the first to bolt, zig-zag,
A treat for the guns and the dogs,
And now any which way, breaking cover,
Too many for the dogs to get them all.

But there was a doe who crouched over
Her young, peeing on her legs in fright,
And held up the tractor.
Even the dogs didn't know
What to do about that.

Cattle Trucks

At the level crossing
As the trucks idle, the
Weinfest band plays the march
It played from the square
And marches on the spot.

Old rolling stock, flügelhorn and
Tuba, doors half open, dark and
Another dark, wheel scrinch and clang,
Old players, too much wine, trumpet
On edge and drum going nowhere.
Not easy for them in this heat,
Muzzy-headed, sweat on valve and mouthpiece,
Sweat in feathered hat, boots in tar,
Steel in the wrong key, sun glint and blind,
Sun bladdered out of shape, heatsway in pylon,
Burnt smell from the track, wires staved high
With octaves as the trucks grind and dawdle.
Too much wine and spent feet, fingers
Missing the stops, heat shapes, heat shimmer,
Dark and another dark, and
'Was nie gesehen nie geschehen'
As the trucks grind and dawdle.

At the level crossing
As the trucks idle, the
Weinfest band plays the march
It played from the square
And marches on the spot.

In the Pub

One of them tells it breakneck,
Left hand out, four fingers, three,
Fist up, thumb wagging, flash of palm
And bang into the right, two hands now,
Brushing, marrying, cutting loose,
Flicking at lip and chin, face alive
With the telling, 'and you'll never
Guess what happened next'.

His friend listens with his eyes,
Doesn't miss a word, keeps the ball
In the air, forearm chop, nose-touch,
Hands in steeple, thumb across cheek,
'Get away, not really? You must be joking'.

And then the punch line,
A blur of hands and faces
And the two of them roar with
Utterly silent laughter.

Out here the two of us yell
Above the yell above the jukebox.
We need words that reach, but the
Words we need make no sense
Unless they're said quietly
Or said by needful arms or
By a hand tracing the
Curve of a cheek.

If You Have a Moment

Think of Telemann.
Twelve children, then
His wife left with a sailor.

A short pause, to air the bed perhaps,
Then another wife and twelve more children.
And through it all, music by the cartload,
Business as usual, so the scholars say,
No move to the minor, no change of key.

Did he notice, do you think,
As he weaned another trio sonata
Or got a fugue walking?
And if he did, just listen to the
Laughter in that avalanche of notes.

Serum

That sudden country terror in
This city flat, as I hold nightshade
Or the wrong amanita, or among
Traffic noise have disturbed an adder
And must stay completely still.

And completely still, let me sit here
A moment and somehow get back and
Watch carefully that leaf caught by
A dam of twigs, turning in the small
Stream, water in a dance of light
On low branches and under sunlit water
The dark bed of last year's leaves.
Let me for a moment be frightened and have
Nothing in my head but the fan-vaulted
Leaf noise and the wood about its business
And the silence and the tiny weir.

Peace

Is not silence.
Is your chair creaking,
A cough, someone on the stair,
Your own breathing.

Silence is station null,
Raging nothing, the hiss
Of lymph, the scream just
Above your range, the high E
That drove Smetana mad.

So hum a bit, drop a pencil,
Talk to yourself, make the most
Of a sneeze, let in all clutter
That underwrites your risky clef.

Scaffolder

Three hundred feet up the cliff
Of Chartres, I bet you sang,
Trusting frayed ropes,
Fashioning a gargoyle from
Your mother-in-law,
Not the plainsong of Perrotin,
But I bet you sang.

Now, balanced up there on
One plank, you lean over
To clamp what doesn't yet ...
Stop you falling ...

Ratchet on ratchet you
Grind down another face and
Once again not Perrotin
On your crackling trannie,
More chance and dance and swing
As you lean out to the last
Inch and lean a bit further
And sing.

Coming of Age

Were you there that morning when,
After all, you were not Beethoven,
Nor even that obscure Finn
With the one song that survives?

Was it a release, a shrug
That was always in the package,
A lifetime's grudge, an illness
Perhaps, a growth that might
Need surgery?

Or were you, like him,
Hard of hearing, or even truant
And not at home that morning?

Let It

A morning like this in your face,
Winter gone, winter with a last kick,
Dare me or go back by the fire,
Wind pinning back feathergrass for
The sun to rape it, cumulus voyaging
The weathercock, roof lichen getting
Richer by the minute, hawk surfing in nothing,
Stag beetle clutching for a hold, shutters
Banging, grass racing raced up the valley,
A morning like this best of all is go
Childhood daft, run and shout back at it,
Sail under bare poles up the sea valley, be
Oakbranch fronting it, see yourself primary,
Brook-washed, nothing left of night but
Drops swaying in thorn hangars, throwing back
All colours the sun is made of.

Hospital Visitors

Their outside rainy smell,
Coats and macs, grumbling
About parking, arranging wet
Feet around the bed, praising
The room, getting out grapes
And flowers, non-looking at the
Tubes and wires; their faces
Celebrate that they are not yet us.

Here in this perpetual Sunday
They are the weekday others,
Glancing at watches instead of
Gauges on their wrists.
Nurse with her face round the
Door sees at once that they
Are not of our Order, have not
Taken the vows of our Order,
Must be let out, allowed down
The corridor, into the lift,
Out into unsterilized rain.

Crutchspeed

Hey hey, I am Toad, escaped by sheer
Cunning from Zimmer prison,
Dot and carry two I am Fangio
Burning up the corridor, accelerating
Past cleaners, getting nosey,
Slamming on brakes at a half-open
Door and the wreck on the bed,
Blocking trolley traffic, chatting up
Nurses, dirt-tracking bends.

Arrested by Sister, I agree
To come quietly.

But, toadlike, I plot.
Tomorrow, moving slowly,
Smiling with pain and
Forgiving them so hard
That they lose interest,
I shall reach those doors,
The lovely clashing doors,
And I shall press the button
For down, and then, heavily
Disguised, I shall scream up
The middle of the Euston Road.

E.F.L.

If it is present
And you are doing it,
The verb stays as it is.
Love.
All you do is
Put yourself in front.

If someone else is doing it,
She, for instance,
Then it changes.
Loves.
You add an S.

If it is to come, then
Whether it is you or she,
It does not change,
But will goes in between
To show that it is coming.

If it is past, you
Simply add a D.
Loved.
That is what changes it from now
And this time it
Does not matter who is speaking.

Mandelbrot

He's a mathematical hero,
He dances the edge between
Infinity and zero,
He's plump and cuddly,
He's the gingerbread man,
And run run as fast as you can,
You won't catch up with
The gingerbread man.

He's mountains, moonscapes.
Seahorses, cacti, zig-zag
Contortions, coastlines,
Snakes, geometric extortions.

If you think you've caught him,
He's best eaten in
Very small portions,
But small is enormous,
Small is his universe,
Small is corridors longer
Than your throat, and
Eat, eat as fast as you can,
You'll never swallow
The gingerbread man.

With the Woolwich

(For Roy Fuller)

And there he stayed, not from cowardice,
Not longing for rescue, but because
He liked it, was good at it, coped
With mortgages, policies, cumulative
Interest, bad debts, dry-rot surveys,
Got on with the nine to five;
Wrote his very own poems, honourably
Laid bare his flank, said something
Utterly singular, never thought it
Was major; admired his betters
With their protective breakdowns;
Was surprised, amused at the Honours;
Coped, as of course he would, with
The Oxford Chair, but probably valued
More highly his seat on the Board.

Blake

From that country
He comes back with wine
That didn't travel, charred
Film, gifts that don't belong.

Head full of sun, like daft
Jimmy down by the pond, he pets
A beetle and jabbers at the face
Of simple water.

What should we make
Of his cupped empty hands,
Words stolen from
A foreign tongue,
Music belled like fever
In his head, in his
Very own tinnitus?

'Do not go gentle into that good night'

Many go screaming to split their
Faces, many racked by nerve-ends
And begging for morphia, or heroes
Reduced to child-babble by those
Behind the lights who want information,
Or those who seek their own dark
Like lovers, or six million, all
Dignity gone, in the Zyklon B showers.

Some mid-family, mid-morning,
Not hearing the crack of the rifle,
Some on cloud walkabout or plotting
Yet more codicils, some long past
Caring when the machine will be cut.

And a lucky few just ebbing and
Knowing it, content that it's over.
Down that beach they go gentle.
Not a bad way to go.

Diatonic

First Bach said all there was to say.

After that it got rough:
The greedy Haydn said it all
And left nothing more to say,
Except of course for Mozart who
Had his own all and hogged it
And left nothing more to say,
That is with the exception of
Beethoven with a different all,
Not leaving much for Schubert
Who, however, said it all,
Leaving nothing more to say.

It was Bach's fault, getting
That near to Heaven and
Leaving nothing more to say.

His ghost in the organ loft is
Chained to the sixteen foot pipe.
Wired up for sound, he must for a
Certain term on earth, listen to Schoenberg,
Berg, Webern, Stockhausen ...
His special punishment is that with
His hands on the manuals, he must say
It all again, but this time unheard.

Amanita Virosa

(commonly known as 'the destroying angel')

Unlike the cobra she is modest,
But surely the promises are given
For that dark marriage in the guts.
No matter, no matter at all that you
Forget the bridal colour, shy among
The oak roots and the sweet smell
As you carried her home.

And the promises are final.
In your raging soil she will plant
A lust bracken, nurse it with her life,
Lie with you more intimate than flesh
And on that rack of orgasm will
Consummate all you have ever wondered
And will in her own time die with you
And give you peace.

At the Ferry

High water, Sir?
Why bless you, no.
High water is when
She's alive and everything
Afloat and tugging right
Up there above the weed
And all broad across and
Craft moving while they can.
It's everyone at it for
An inch under their keel
And get out of my way and
Bugger the old hulks
Groaning upright and mind
The spikes on the bottom.
It's when she's at the
Step you're standing on.
And look you down,
She's long gone from that.

Notre Dame des Touristes

Seriously ...
Yes I know, heavily forgiven, the run
Past the buy-a-candle nun
And that smell of perfumed dust
And in latin you musn't or you must
And swords and flags, military honours,
Sideshows, trophies, sugary madonnas,
Flagstoned alleys deep sunk
In urns and bones and marble junk
And, explaining what it all means,
That neutered wailing behind the screens.

Yes, it's easy to sneer,
But seriously, have a look,
What is going on in here?
Once through the door,
What are we doing,
What is it for?

Japanese, all ten of it, searches guidebook,
African girl gives me sidelook,
Germans stare up in german at stained glass,
Ici Cook lectures his class,
Lapps or Finns or whatever they are
Think there might be a mediaeval bar,
Fifty children in orderly rank
Almost as solemn as being in a bank,
The whisperers, the confident talkers,
The finger-in-index walkers,
The newmade rich, the newmade poor,
The lost in transit, the solitary gawpers,
The shepherded old, the knowers of church
Lore, ladies from Chicago and more
And more and more.

Please, seriously ...
Museum, terminus, lost property hall?
Cemetery, opera house, souvenir stall,
Chantry for dressed-up sycophants,
Dried-out badger invested by ants,
Humped carcase left where it died,
Huge and strange to the insects inside?
Mitre and aumbry, altar and cup,
Is it best seen the other way up,
Should one hang from a corbel, batlike, aloof,
Is that why others are crawling on the roof?
Could we for a moment turn it on its side,
Is there something it wants to hide?
Does it all belong, like so much in this town,
To that old woman, crouched down
In a pew, not mourning the dead,
But covertly eating sausage and bread?

Out now.

High heel, bare foot, black shoe and sandal,
And here's the nun again with her candle.
Forgiveness again and behind the flame a
Smiling frown. Surely not, not by ten thousand
Hail Mary's, not by her vows, her rosary and gown,
Not surely an invitation to
Burn the place down?

Place de l'Opéra

What can it be like as she walks
Within that sudden ripeness, to feel
The upward tug of a blouse and air
That crowds to touch her?

And on the headlong journey
Did they tell her of us,
Like the sun from its kennel,
Her treacherous court?

Oh there will be time,
There will be time among
The boulevard tables.
For now, let her be first ever,
feather-light, learning
As a flower learns.

Coffee at Montségur

From snowline up another thousand feet
They hauled stone and wood, held
A plumbline still against the northeaster,
Levelled blocks of half a ton, somehow
Jacked up roof-timbers, carried up
The old and children, animals, fodder,
Monitored springwater by the jug.

They believed the intolerable:
Since God is good and cannot make evil,
But there is evil, then Satan
Must have his territory here
On Earth inviolate.

They never harmed an ant, had no army,
Were called in slum and hall alike
'The good people'.
Maybe it was the goodness that
Made Rome murderous.

Six months of siege, with
What that must have meant,
Before the trebuchets broke
The walls.

Just over there, quite near
This sunny coffee terrace,
Two hundred of them were burned
Who refused to recant.

Rome won, but it made a mistake.
It should have razed every stone
And never left that jagged shell
Still pointing upwards.

Just before the end, so the story goes,
Four of them, chosen by lot, were sent
Out secretly and were never traced.

May they have multiplied.
May they be written in many
Most ordinary faces.

Bon Marché

In the market of Rue Montorgeuil
I saw the back of her head, saw her
Turning and I ran like mad, leapt
Stalls of cêpes, girolles, endive,
Salsify, mounds of fish, oysters,
Cheeses, sheeps' brains, pigs' guts,
Cows' wombs, things pulled off rocks,
Stuff from birds' livers, lobsters still
Moving ...
Ducked under carts, dodged among legs,
Feet, offal, rotten fruit, vaulted barrows
While they yelled get him, only thirty
Francs a kilo, stop him, bargain you
Dream of, choose now, pin him down, take
Your pick, never better, only five francs
For a couple of wings, don't move an inch,
Bargain of a lifetime, just look at
What you're getting, choose now,
Never better ...

Museums are safe-houses, ten francs
For warm and dry, sin-free, peering over
Calm shoulders ...

But here in the Musée Picasso something
Grabs my arm and it's frogmarch, weaseltrot,
Toadsprint, ratgallop past old drivelling men,
Garrotted cockerels, pots that are birds,
Wire cats, straw donkeys — all with eyes toward
The dead end where she waits to turn her head.

Castle Museum at Foix

Here in the glass cases are
What they used
And you see straight away
The imagination, the care
That went into them.

This one has a twisted
Point for the thrust and a claw
To pull out what guts it can get.
Here, to smash in a face, is a
Spiked ball like a flail and
Next to it a curved blade,
Barbed in the outer edge:
And all of them good to hold,
Balanced, crafted for a grip.

Absent from the cases are the
Screaming, the guts hanging out,
The dead-not-yet-dead and shoulders,
Arms, hands.

Big hands they must have had
For these parodies of ploughshare
And sickle, this good steel that
Might have peopled a field with wheat.

Centre Ville

Shut in its very own afternoon,
The Place Gambetta debates
Where to let the sun in.
Not urgent, but between oldies
Hunched together in this heat,
A matter of priorities and angles.

A mansarde, five narrow stories up,
Kindled as if someone still lives there,
Lichen gilded on a roof, the Chemist's
Window made suddenly special,
The peeling greek pediment, special,
The washed-out Maiso De Be.

Down here two old ladies,
Sisters maybe, manage not to notice
Powerbiked bloods outside the bar
Or their girls or foreign us.
Among potted plants stacked on
The pavement they greet serious
People in from the villages and
Serious too the pigeon-shitted General
And serious his dry trough for horses.

Now, but not too hard, the sun is
Selling three second-hand tractors
While we, foreign as we came,
Mapread what kilometres we
Can make by dusk.

Cicadas

When the fridge shudders
And air has to be reached for
And ants stay down in their
Cool halls and the thrush
Leans dumb against a branch,
When flies sweat on the tiles
And not one leaf moves,
Not the slightest top of grass:
Then, on the cue of silence,
They start.

First one,
A tuning scrape,
Then six with their own
Sprung rhythms off the beat
Jazzing and jigging
Praising heat and now treefulls,
Colonies of wrong-footed sambas,
Fugal gigues and by your leave
Your high and dry Highness, the
Syncopated smoochy, the
In-and-out dizzy, the dry-tongued
Scrape-your-legs lie with it,
Come and get it, die with it
And all, all in the key of dryness:
There never was rain,
We know why the spring dried,
There never can be rain,
We know why the well dried.

They watch as, in this
Lucky pause between the centuries,
We turn on a tap.
They watch the hose kick
And see its nozzle, what is
Spilled, how quickly earth
Darkens and air suddenly
Is leaf and root.

Masterclass

The dawn Paganinis, the cadenzas,
Anything with just a little talent,
All that I can script into my dream.

But on your sheet
There are just two notes.
A descending fourth with
Three semi-tones in between.
Cuck, miss three, coo.

Read it again.
Cuck, down we go,
Miss three,
Coo.

Can't you get it right at four
In the morning, you tin-eared
Myopic feathered nit?
Take it slowly: cuck, pause,
Count the semi-tones, coo.

What dream would be proof against
Your cuck-sharp, cuck count two,
Cuck nothing, cuck missed it,
Cuck sorry ......?

St. Francis in Tarn-et-Garonne

Brother mosquito, airframe that
Art so light, singing high in
The dark with thy needle and
I already wounded with thy love.

Brother mosquito, prayer has
Given us the electric light
And this holy can of Flytox.

Brother mosquito, let us
Be cheerful and praise God.
Soon thou shalt be one with Him,
Or, if my aim is marred by error,
One with me again.

Downhill

You, bulge in my daughter-in-law,
Plotting for me a new name, one
That jerks down the sun, boots out
Afternoon, dumps me, gummy-eyed,
Continent with effort, drivelling
On the evening bench.

Soon we'll be simple together,
Learn about milk and fingers,
Be prammed to sleep in the park,
Be washed, coaxed, put to bed,
While you remember what I forget
And we play don't look, peep-bo
At being born and being dead.

Bardon Hill

'Beorg Dun', so the books say,
But for us it was Bear Den
Where the last one in England
Was caught and killed.
When we knew it as kids there was
Still a cave we kept away from.

And like kids we listened to
The very last of Charnwood,
Oak and beech left to fight it out
As they always had, trees we could
Lose ourselves in, naves, transepts
And cloisters, fan-vaulting in that
Other older canon with its
Discipline of fall and hurt
And heard the thrush echoing off
High tracery. We could have
Shown you among floors of mast and
Acorn the special leaning old,
The ivy-sick, the dead prone
With their warrior ants and the
Young grasping for space, like
Us with their murderous secrets.

Bardon

Old Row and New Row
Dumped parallel on meadows.
Four rooms and up the yard
Squares of yellow newspaper on
A nail in the lysolled ashpit.
Oilstove smell and the forbidden
Front room with wedding tongs and shovel
And the framed dead, still camera-shy.

Two rows with allotments down
To the sidings and a clenched bell
In the single shop.

A quarry village, there for the quarry,
But they noticed harvest, knew the names
Of plants, watched the sky, talked
Of their spuds and marrows, could
Not cross a field but they saw
A crow or a hawk or crunched
A wheat-ear in their hands.

The Hall

Three gables built from quarry profits,
Branches picking at slates, shuttered
Windows, briars like your thumb,
An echoing place for rooks.

Both sons lost on the Somme.
We used to bunk up the wall
And bet which room she lived in.

She caught us scrumping once
And shook her stick.
For a moment she smiled
Before we bolted.

Countryman

A quiet man, he never
Got the mud off.

First it was Charnwood loam
And with it he never forgot,
Under his back, the feel of
Hay that wasn't baled,
Or looking up at an owl-brood
In the rafters, hearing a rat
Building its winter, seeing the
Flattened poppies, the vetch and
Bindweed in barley that failed.

Then it was the clay of the Somme
And with it the language of that
Other harvest that he never could
Say aloud, denied he knew it,
Tried to forget where it was from.

He was proud of our London semi-D
With its inside loo.
A quiet man, but Fridays he became
Restless, made sure the car was ready
For another journey north to
Where the barn was now a road-house
And his cousins still talked of barley
As he took me, piggy-back, along
The edges of fields.

Whist

That afternoon at seventy six,
Never having had much wrong with him,
He fainted in the middle of a hand.
An aortic aneurism that chose to burst
Before all the trumps were out.

Would it have been better for the
Shy two of us to have a little time?
Would we have had the words to say it?

More to the point, I think he
Held all the cards that afternoon.
He was dealt the suit he wanted,
Holding it fan-wise, hearing
His ordinary friends talking
And a sudden quiet exit.

Aunt Nell

Every Christmas there was argument
About who would get her.

Her year was the blind in India,
African lepers, drought in the Sudan.

Early in December she sent out
Cards painted by the foot.

As she pulled crackers, she smiled
Sadly from under her paper hat,
Wanting us to enjoy it.
We hoped she wasn't fondly looking
As we opened our presents.

Aunt Nell's Legacy

All I remember is that the best cups
Came out of the top cupboard and
She was allowed to hold one
With tea in it.

Nobody said anything, but I
Knew that suddenly she was
Richer than the Queen.

The next time she came
It was the cups we always had.
I was glad about that because
They were bigger for the tea
And I didn't want her to spoil
The one dress she always wore.

Aunt Nell and the Album

Nearly always she's at the back,
Half a hat, a someone behind
The other wide smiles.

But there is one, snapped before
She knew it, watching my exultant
Son, the first ever to walk on legs,
She exultant too, with a face
That must once have been open
Like the primrose.

Behind her, not caught by the camera,
Is never-came who years before would
Have cupped her face in his hands
And never let it change.

Uncle George

He came just once, when I was three.
He laughed a lot with a big face
And all the rest were quiet.

Aunt Nell knew about him, but she
Always went behind a smile.

Once or twice he sent presents
That must have cost a bomb.
We never thanked him. He didn't
Seem to have an address.

Aunt Nell would say, forgivingly,
'People have their little weaknesses.'

When the family said anything, it said
It was a family that didn't have
People like Uncle George in it.

There was a snap in the album.
Not, like all the others, with a
Name and a date. Someone with mum's
Look when she was hiding something.

And an Aunt Nell postcard and dad
Walking up and down with his toast
Saying: 'Oh no, not again.'

For the Record

We never saw them kiss.
He awkwardly tried it sometimes,
But she always had things to do.
No business of ours that earlier
There must have been kisses.

And the same privacy when,
For a day, they were apart,
And were that much less.

Dying, he tried a daft sorry
For going first.

She dealt with the funeral,
Became Grannie who
Got on with it.
No business of ours what
She waited for, sorting through
Dresses like a nervous girl.

Actuarial You

As you pedal in the gym, chew your
Sunflower seed, heavily non-smoke
And count the untouched dry martinis,
You deserve a look ahead.

There will be the good days when,
Nappy-changed, you can be coaxed out
Into air by voices you almost remember
As they point out rose-blur, willow-blur
And the scraping noise of thrush.

Or, who knows, this one twisted among
Cushions or this one muttering at hands
Can be you, clenched like a limpet to the
Extra day that makes it all worthwhile.

Citadel

Hip grinding in socket,
Cataract gaining, one ear dead,
Breath that has to be reached for
And back to nappies.

All that she deals with
more clinically than us.

But, for fear, hiding her teeth under
The pillow, dressing before dawn to get
The kingcups down the quicksand corridor,
Promises made to lop-haired Nessie and
Pin on my bride-veil before he dies.
Knowing, knowing it will come again
And the centre can't be trusted.

Like an old jungle fighter, that
Has her at bay, eyes tired of looking out
And terrified of looking in.

Care Home

It's one of her brooch days.
Wary of us, she twists it
In her lap, clenches it for
Secrets we musn't find out.

She knows we're here with
Our flowers and fruit,
Caring us who staked her out
In this house of the dying.
But it's a brooch day,
Set aside for the puzzling
Shapes of bitterness and,
Through the rime of cataract,
A giving that won't come clear
And, locked in her fingers, a caring
That seemed careless at the time.

In There

Every now and then one of them
Doesn't come down to claim
Her usual chair.
It's all dealt with quietly
And Matron is smiling.
The rest of them try and think
Who it was that sat there yesterday.

You don't ask questions here
For nobody is listening, but
Old Millie yells from her zimmer frame

'Come in number six, your time
Is up'.
And then like a child in tears,
'I wish it was me'.

Wheelchair Meeting

Not much left to spare, but there is
The companionship of saying nothing.

Parked out here in the sun, each
Probably understands that
The other is there.

And, more than that, each may feel
That if words could be said and heard,
They would be the right words, probably.

And perhaps even more, that in and out
Of time, there was, could have been
That other meeting under these clenched
Knuckles of wisteria with their slippery
Load of memory.